teacher's friend publications

June

a creative idea book
for the
elementary teacher

written and illustrated
by
Karen Sevaly

Copyright © 1988
Teacher's Friend Publications, Inc.
All rights reserved
Printed in the United States of America
Published by Teacher's Friend Publications, Inc.
7407 Orangewood Drive, Riverside, CA 92504
ISBN 0-943263-09-3

TO TEACHERS AND CHILDREN EVERYWHERE

Table of Contents

Making the Most of It!

WHAT IS IN
THIS BOOK:

You will find the following in each monthly idea book from Teacher's Friend Publications:

1. A calendar listing every day of the month with a classroom idea.

2. At least four new student awards to be sent home to parents.

3. Three new bookmarks that can be used in your school library or given to students by you as "Super Student Awards."

4. Numerous bulletin board ideas and patterns pertaining to the particular month.

5. Easy to make craft ideas related to the monthly holidays.

6. Dozens of activities emphasizing not only the obvious holidays but also chapters related to such subjects as; Oceanography and Reptiles.

7. Crossword puzzles, word finds, creative writing pages, booklet covers and much more.

8. Scores of classroom management techniques, the newest and the best.

HOW TO USE
THIS BOOK:

Every page of this book may be duplicated for individual classroom use.

Some pages are meant to be used as duplicating masters and used as student work sheets. Other pages may be copied onto construction paper or used as they are.

If you have access to a print shop, you will find that many pages work well when printed on index paper. This type of paper takes crayons and felt markers well and is sturdy enough to last and last. The wheel pattern and bookmarks are two items that work particularly well on index paper.

Lastly, some pages are meant to be enlarged with an overhead or opaque projector. When we say enlarge, we mean it! Think BIG! Three, four or even five feet is great! Try using colored butcher paper or poster board so you don't spend all your time coloring.

ADDING THE COLOR:

Putting the color to finished items can be a real bother to teachers in a rush. Try these ideas:

1. On small areas, water color markers work great. If your area is rather large switch to crayons or even colored chalk or pastels.

   (Don't worry, lamination or a spray fixative will keep the color on the work and off of you. No laminator or fixative? That's okay, a little hair spray will do the trick.)

2. The quickest method of coloring large items is to simply start with colored paper. (Poster board, butcher paper and large construction paper work well.) Add a few dashes of a contrasting colored marker or crayon and you will have it made.

3. Try cutting character eyes, teeth, etc. from white typing paper and gluing them in place. These features will really stand out and make your bulletin boards come alive.

   For special effects add real buttons or lace. Metallic paper looks great on stars and belt buckles, too.

LAMINATORS:

If you have access to a roll laminator you already know how fortunate you are. They are priceless when it comes to saving time and money. Try these ideas:

1. You can laminate more than just classroom posters and construction paper. Try various kinds of fabric, wall paper and gift wrapping. You'll be surprised at the great combinations you come up with.

   Laminated classified ads can be used to cut headings for current event bulletin boards. Colorful gingham fabric makes terrific cut letters or scalloped edging. You might even try burlap! It looks terrific on a fall bulletin board.

   (You can even make professional looking bookmarks with laminated fabric or burlap. They are great gift ideas.)

2. Felt markers and laminated paper or fabric can work as a team. Just make sure the markers you use are permanent and not water based. Oops, make a mistake! That's okay. Put a little ditto fluid on a tissue, rub across the mark and presto, it's gone! (Dry transfer markers work great on lamination, too.)

LAMINATORS:
(continued)

3. Laminating cut-out characters can be tricky. If you have enlarged an illustration onto poster board, simply laminate first and then cut it out with an art knife. (Just make sure the laminator is plenty hot.)

One problem may arise when you paste an illustration onto poster board and laminate the finished product. If your paste-up does not cover 100% of the illustration, the poster board may separate from it after laminating. To avoid this problem, paste your illustration onto poster board that measures slightly larger. This way, the lamination will help hold down your illustration.

4. Have you ever laminated student-made place mats, crayon shavings, tissue paper collages, or dried flowers? You'll be amazed at the variety of creative things that can be laminated and used in the classroom, or as take-home gifts.

DITTO MASTERS:

Many of the pages in this book can be made into masters for duplicating. Try some of these ideas for best results:

1. When using new masters, turn down the pressure on the duplicating machine. As the copies become light, increase the pressure. This will get longer wear out of both the master and the machine.

2. If the print from the back side of your original comes through the front when making a master or photocopy, slip a sheet of black construction paper behind the sheet. This will mask the unwanted black lines and create a much better copy.

3. Trying to squeeze one more run out of that worn master can be frustrating. Try lightly spraying the inked side of the master with hair spray. For some reason, this helps the master put out those few extra copies.

4. Several potential masters in this book contain instructions for the teacher. Simply cover the type with correction fluid or a small slip of paper before duplicating.

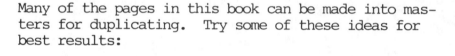

BULLETIN BOARDS:

Creating clever bulletin boards for your classroom need not take fantastic amounts of time and money. With a little preparation and know-how you can have different boards each month with very little effort. Try some of these ideas:

1. Background paper should be put up only once a year. Choose colors that can go with many themes and holidays. A black butcher paper background will look terrific with springtime butterflies or a spooky Halloween display.

2. Butcher paper is not the only thing that can be used to cover the back of your board. You might like to try the classified ad section of the local newspaper for a current events board. Or how about colored burlap? Just fold it up at the end of the year to reuse again.

3. Wallpaper is another great background cover. Discontinued rolls can be purchased for next to nothing at discount hardware stores. Most can be wiped clean and will not fade like construction paper. (Do not glue wallpaper directly to the board, just staple or pin in place.)

ON-GOING BULLETIN BOARDS:

Creating the on-going bulletin board can be easy. Give one of these ideas a try.

1. Choose one board to be a calendar display. Students can change this monthly. They can do the switching of dates, month titles and holiday symbols. Start the year with a great calendar board and with a few minor changes each month it will add a sparkle to the classroom.

2. A classroom tree bulletin board is another one that requires very little attention after September. Cut a large bare tree from brown butcher paper and display it in the center of the board. (Wood-grained adhesive paper makes a great tree, also.) Children can add fall leaves, flowers, apples, Christmas ornaments, birds, valentines, etc., to change the appearance each month.

**ON-GOING
BULLETIN BOARDS:**
(continued)

3. Birthday bulletin boards, classroom helpers, school announcement displays and reading group charts can all be created once before school starts and changed monthly with very little effort. With all these on-going ideas, you'll discover that all that bulletin board space seems smaller than you thought.

**LETTERING AND
HEADINGS:**

Not every school has a letter machine that produces perfect 2" or 4" letters from construction paper. (There is such a thing, you know.) The rest of us will just have to use the old stencil and scissor method. But wait, there is an easier way!

1. Don't cut individual letters. They are difficult to pin up straight, anyway. Instead, hand print bulletin board titles and headings onto strips of colored paper. When it is time for the board to come down, simply roll it up to use again next year.

   Use your imagination. Try cloud shapes and cartoon bubbles. They will all look great.

2. Hand lettering is not that difficult, even if your printing is not up to penmanship standards. Print block letters with a felt marker. Draw big dots at the ends of each letter. This will hide any mistakes and add a charming touch to the overall effect.

LETTERING AND
HEADINGS:
(continued)

If you are still afraid about free handing it, try this nifty idea: Cut a strip of poster board about 28" X 6". Down the center of the strip cut a window with an art knife measuring 20" X 2". There you have it, a perfect stencil for any lettering job. All you do is write your letters with a felt marker within the window slot. Don't worry about uniformity, just fill up the entire window heighth with your letters. Move your poster board strip along as you go. The letters will always remain straight and even because the poster board window is straight.

3. If you must cut individual letters, use this idea:

Cut numerous sheets of construction paper into 4½" X 6" squares. (Laminate first if you can.) Cut letters as shown in the illustration. No need to measure, irregular letters will look creative not messy.

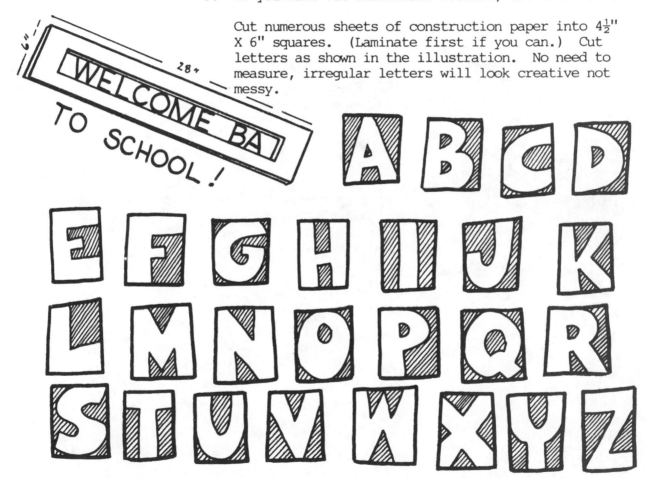

Notes

Calendar

- JUNE CALENDAR AND ACTIVITIES

- CALENDAR TOPPERS

- BLANK CALENDAR

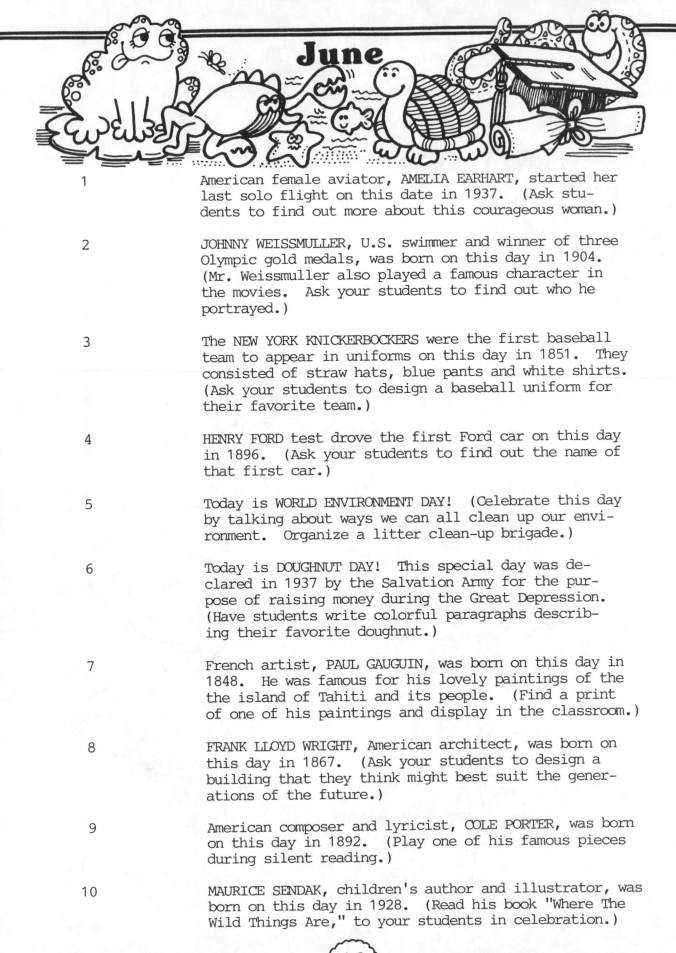

June

1   American female aviator, AMELIA EARHART, started her last solo flight on this date in 1937. (Ask students to find out more about this courageous woman.)

2   JOHNNY WEISSMULLER, U.S. swimmer and winner of three Olympic gold medals, was born on this day in 1904. (Mr. Weissmuller also played a famous character in the movies. Ask your students to find out who he portrayed.)

3   The NEW YORK KNICKERBOCKERS were the first baseball team to appear in uniforms on this day in 1851. They consisted of straw hats, blue pants and white shirts. (Ask your students to design a baseball uniform for their favorite team.)

4   HENRY FORD test drove the first Ford car on this day in 1896. (Ask your students to find out the name of that first car.)

5   Today is WORLD ENVIRONMENT DAY! (Celebrate this day by talking about ways we can all clean up our environment. Organize a litter clean-up brigade.)

6   Today is DOUGHNUT DAY! This special day was declared in 1937 by the Salvation Army for the purpose of raising money during the Great Depression. (Have students write colorful paragraphs describing their favorite doughnut.)

7   French artist, PAUL GAUGUIN, was born on this day in 1848. He was famous for his lovely paintings of the the island of Tahiti and its people. (Find a print of one of his paintings and display in the classroom.)

8   FRANK LLOYD WRIGHT, American architect, was born on this day in 1867. (Ask your students to design a building that they think might best suit the generations of the future.)

9   American composer and lyricist, COLE PORTER, was born on this day in 1892. (Play one of his famous pieces during silent reading.)

10   MAURICE SENDAK, children's author and illustrator, was born on this day in 1928. (Read his book "Where The Wild Things Are," to your students in celebration.)

11	Famous oceanographer and author, JACQUES COUSTEAU, was born on this day in 1910. (Have your students write an imaginative story about the adventures of his ship, the "Calypso.")
12	The author of "Diary of a Young Girl," ANNE FRANK, was born on this day in 1929. (Older children may find her story very interesting.)
13	THURGOOD MARSHALL, the first black Supreme Court Justice, was appointed to the bench on this day in 1967 by President Johnson. (Ask your students to find out the procedures for appointing a Supreme Court Justice.)
14	Today is FLAG DAY in the United States! (Ask students to list ways we can all show our respect for our flag.)
15	Today is SMILE POWER DAY! (Celebrate the day by asking students to tell their favorite joke or write a comical poem or story.)
16	Soviet cosmonaut, VALENTINA TERESHKOVA, became the first woman to travel into space in 1963. (Ask students to find out the name of the first U.S. woman astronaut.)
17	The first REPUBLICAN NATIONAL CONVENTION was held on this day in 1856 in Philadelphia, Pennsylvania. (Ask students to find out the purpose of political conventions or design a campaign button.)
18	Today is INTERNATIONAL PICNIC DAY! (Ask each child to bring a sack lunch and visit a local park during the school lunch break.)
19	The comic strip "GARFIELD" appeared for the first time on this date in 1978. (Ask your students to create their own comic strip character.)
20	SAMUEL MORSE was granted a patent for the telegraph on this day in 1840. (Display the Morse Code on the class chalkboard and have the children learn to tap out their own names.)
21	Today marks the first day of SUMMER! It is also the longest day of the year. (Ask older students to find out why this fact is true.)

22   On this day in 1970, the VOTING AGE in the United States was changed from 21 years of age to 18. (Ask your students views on the legal ages for driving, drinking and voting.)

23   WILMA RUDOLPH, winner of three Olympic gold medals at the 1960 Olympic Games, was born on this day in 1940. (Ask your students to find out more about this talented woman athlete.)

24   RADAR was first used on this date in 1930 to detect airplanes. (Ask your students to find what the acronym R-A-D-A-R signifies.)

25   GEORGE CUSTER and his troops were defeated at the BATTLE OF LITTLE BIGHORN on this day in 1876. (Ask your students to find out what state is the home of this famous battle site.)

26   On this day in 1870, the world's first BOARDWALK in Atlantic City, New Jersey, was opened. (Ask your students to locate Atlantic City on the classroom map.)

27   HELEN KELLER, American author and lecturer, was born on this date in 1880. (Tell your students about this remarkable woman or read to them the book "The Miracle Worker.")

28   The TREATY OF VERSAILLES, ending World War I, was signed on this day in 1919. (Older children may like to locate Versailles on a European map.)

29   France annexes the island of TAHITI on this day in 1880. (Ask your students to find Tahiti on the classroom map.)

30   The FISH AND WILDLIFE SERVICE was established on this day in 1940. (Have your students investigate different career opportunities related to this service.)

REMEMBER......

FATHER'S DAY is always the third Sunday in June.

JUNE

June

sun	mon	tue	wed	thu	fri	sat

June Activities

- SUMMER FUN

- AWARDS AND BOOKMARKS

- PENCIL TOPPERS

- CERTIFICATES

- PROMOTIONAL MORTARBOARDS

- SUMMER VISOR

Summer Fun

ACTIVITY 1

FIND THESE SUMMER ACTIVITIES:

cook	skate
bike	garden
sleep	explore
picnic	boat
fish	swim
camp	play
hike	sports
sew	

```
S C V G F S W I M K L O P L K J H F T Y
L A W E D F R S D R F T L D E R F G H Y
E S C O O K S D F G T Y A D S P O R T S
E S W E R A E S W D F R Y W S T Y U I O
P A E D R F W E X P L O R E D T Y U K M
I S W G A R D E N D G T Y H B O A T E R
C W Q E R T Y U A W E R T Y H G F D S T
N F R T Y U H J H D F T Y G H U I J K L
I D R F G T I F F I S H F T Y U I O P V
C B I K E D K V G T Y H N M K I O L R E
A X C G T Y E C A M P D V G T Y H N M J
A W E D S C F R T G B H Y U J M N K I O
A S D F G T Y H J K I O S K A T E D R T
X C Z V B G F D S A Z X B N M J K H F D
```

ACTIVITY 2

COMPLETE THIS SUMMER CROSSWORD PUZZLE.

DOWN

1. A water sport

2. You should always look before you _ _ _ _ into the water!

3. To keep your head above water and remain very still.

ACROSS

4. Something wet.

5. All swimmers must have strong _ _ _ _.

6. Swimmers kick with their _ _ _ _.

7. Someone who watches and saves swimmers.

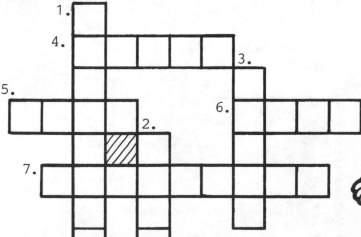

SWIMMING RULES

1. Always swim in areas supervised by an adult or lifeguard.

2. Always check to see how deep the water is before going in.

3. Always walk, never run around a swimming pool.

4. Play gently in the pool. Never be rough or dunk your friends.

5. Never cry for help unless you need it.

JUNE

Awards

_____
Name

FLEW HIGH TODAY!

_____

_____

Name

WAS A GREAT TEAM
PLAYER TODAY!

_____   _____
Teacher   Date

_____
Name

WAS SURE AND STEADY
AT SCHOOL TODAY!

_____

_____

_____   _____
Teacher   Date

_____
Name

CAUGHT A WORLD OF LEARNING
TODAY!

_____

_____

_____   _____
Teacher   Date

JUNE

Pencil Toppers

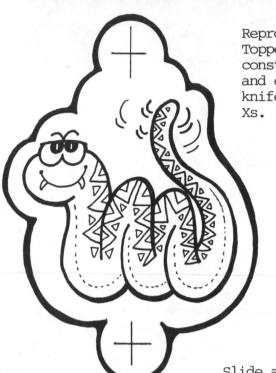

Reproduce these "Pencil Toppers" onto index or construction paper. Color and cut out. Use an art knife to cut through the Xs.

Slide a pencil through both Xs, as shown.

Use as classroom, holiday or birthday treats.

JUNE

Bookmarks

Dive
into the
Library
this
Summer!

Reptiles

Jump ahead this
summer.... READ!

JUNE

CERTIFICATE OF
Recognition

This certificate is presented to

_____

in recognition of

_____

_____

Date _____

CERTIFICATE OF MERIT

is awarded this certificate

in recognition of

CERTIFICATE OF
Achievement

This award of distinction is presented to

_____

in recognition of

_____

_____
Date

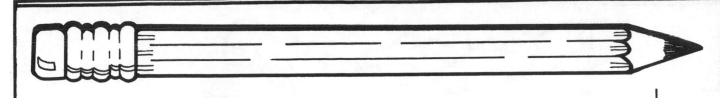

CERTIFICATE OF Participation

has participated with distinction in

_____

TEACHER

PRINCIPAL

JUNE

Certificate
of
Appreciation

given to

_____

in appreciation

for the valuable contribution

_____

Our sincere gratitude is extended to you

on this date, _____

Promotional Mortarboards

Children will love wearing this simple to make mortarboard on the last day of school or during a promotional program.

Cut a long strip of black construction or butcher paper approximately 6" X 22". Wrap the paper around the child's head and staple the ends together to fit.

Now, fold the paper in half and cut a "V", as shown, with a pair of scissors. Next, make several cuts along the top edge and fold them outward.

Place a square piece of black poster-board, (about 10" X 10") onto the folded flaps and glue in place. Glue a black button to the center of the mortarboard and let it dry over night.

The next day, make a tassle from colored yarn and carefully tie it to the button.

Name

PROMOTIONAL NAME TAGS

Your students will be proud to wear these fun name tags on the last day of school. They are especially meaning-ful to elementary students who are being promoted to the junior high school.

The students can color them with crayons or markers.

Visor

Copy this "Have a Great Summer!" visor onto sturdy index or construction paper. Children can do the coloring.

Punch holes at both ends and attach string elastic or mailing string. (With elastic, students can easily remove the visors without retying.)

Have a great SUMMER!

Flag Day

- HISTORY OF OUR FLAG

- "OLD GLORY"

- RESPECTING OUR FLAG

- PLEDGE OF ALLEGIANCE

- PROUD OF MY COUNTRY

33

Flag Day

On Sunday, June 14, 1885, a young schoolmaster named Bernard Cigrand held a birthday party for the 108th birthday of the American flag.

All the people of his hometown, Waubeka, Wisconsin, were invited to the celebration. The school house was decorated with the colors red, white and blue and homemade flags were displayed everywhere. His pupils, dressed in their Sunday best, recited patriotic poems and told stories about the American flag. A poem by Francis Scott Key entitled "The Star-Spangled Banner" was also included. A large cake was served along with refreshing lemonade. At the end of the celebration, everyone joined in a pledge of loyalty to the flag.

After this special day, Cigrand devoted a great deal of his time to reminding people to honor our flag. He wrote letters to statesmen and made numerous speeches. He became known as the father of Flag Day.

In 1916, President Woodrow Wilson officially proclaimed June 14th to be observed throughout the United States as "Flag Day." Every year, since that time, flags are flown on all civic buildings and many schools participate in special programs. It's a time to honor our country's symbol and to feel proud to be an American.

THE HISTORY OF OUR FLAG

The original flag of the United States was raised for the first time on June 14, 1777. It consisted of thirteen stripes, representing the original thirteen colonies and thirteen stars, one for each state of the union.

After the signing of the Declaration of Independence, in 1776, the Continental Congress decided they needed a national flag to symbolize the unity of their new country.

According to legend, a committee led by George Washington requested a woman from Philadelphia, named Betsy Ross, to design and make the first United States flag. It is believed that she chose the colors red, white and blue. Later these colors became a part of the Great Seal of the United States. It is said that the color red stands for courage and hardiness, white symbolizes purity and innocence and blue represents perserverance and justice.

FIRST OFFICIAL FLAG - JUNE 14, 1777

The Continental Congress created a resolution that states: "The flag of the United States shall be 13 stripes, alternating red and white and the union be 13 stars, white in a blue field, representing the new constellation." This flag is also known as the "Betsy Ross" flag.

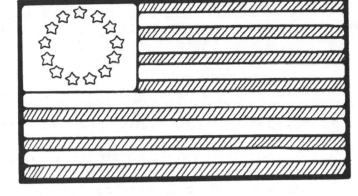

THE FIFTEEN STRIPE FLAG - 1794

On January 13, 1794, the Congress recognized the new states of Vermont and Kentucky and voted to add two stripes and two stars to the flag. This is the flag that inspired Francis Scott Key to write our National Anthem. This flag remained unchanged until 1818.

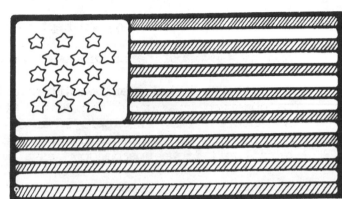

THE NATIONAL FLAG OF 1818

Twenty states had joined the Union by 1818. On April 18th, the Congress voted to have the flag display 13 alternate red and white stripes representing the original 13 states and each new state would be recognized by adding a new star.

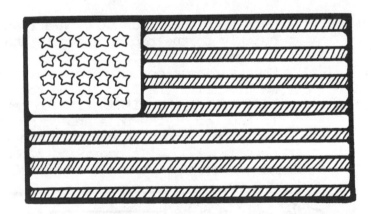

OUR PRESENT NATIONAL FLAG

The flag steadily changed between 1818 and 1912 as more states were added to the Union. From 1912 to 1959, there were 48 stars on the blue field. Alaska became our 49th state in 1959 and then in 1960 Hawaii became our 50th state. With 50 stars and 13 stripes, "Old Glory" as we know it, came into being.

Respecting Our Flag

1. Our flag should always be treated in a respectful manner.

2. Always stand when our flag is represented in a parade or carried in an honor guard. Hats should also be removed when our flag is presented.

3. Our flag should only be flown from sunrise to sunset. It may be flown at night only when it is properly lighted.

4. Our flag should be stored and displayed in a way that will keep it clean, dry and free from harm. It should never be displayed in extremely bad weather.

5. Our flag must always be kept from touching the floor or the ground.

6. Our flag must never be used as a decoration or a costume.

7. Nothing should ever be placed on or above our flag.

8. When our flag is displayed in a window or on a wall, always keep the union of stars to the top and the observer's left. The flag is only flown upside down as a distress signal, a call for help.

9. When our flag becomes worn beyond repair, destroy it in a dignified manner by burning it.

10. When displaying our flag on a flag pole, always raise the flag quickly to the top of the pole and lower it slowly.

11. When a famous person passes away, we often display our flag at half-mast. Hoist the flag to the top of the pole and slowly lower it to half-mast. When it is time to take it down, raise the flag again to the top of the pole and bring it down slowly. It always takes two people to raise or lower the flag correctly.

FOLDING OUR FLAG

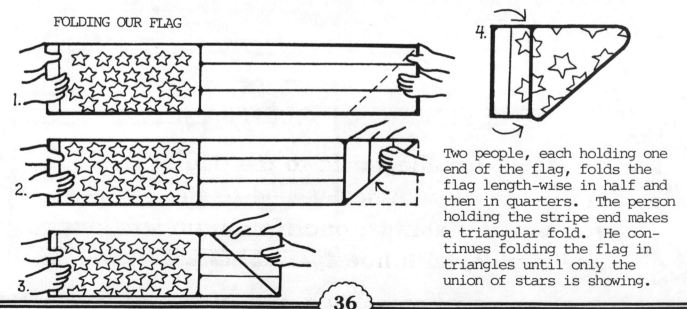

Two people, each holding one end of the flag, folds the flag length-wise in half and then in quarters. The person holding the stripe end makes a triangular fold. He continues folding the flag in triangles until only the union of stars is showing.

THE PLEDGE OF ALLEGIANCE

"I pledge allegiance to the flag of the
United States of America and to the Republic
for which it stands, one Nation under God,
indivisible, with liberty and justice for all."

JUNE

Proud of My Country!

JUNE

Father's Day

- FATHER'S DAY SUGGESTIONS

- FATHER'S DAY POCKET

- FATHER'S DAY CARD

- MY DAD IS SPECIAL

- FATHER'S DAY CERTIFICATES

- CREATIVE WRITING

- A LETTER TO DAD

Father's Day

In 1909, Louise Smart Dodd of Spokane, Washington, encouraged the congregation of her church to devote a special day to fathers. Louise was very close to her own father. Her mother had died when Louise was a small child and her father had lovingly raised her and her five brothers. Louise wanted to honor her own father by dedicating a special day to all fathers.

Several years later, President Coolidge recommended that a "Father's Day" be nationally observed. The third Sunday in June was selected for this special day. Today, children in both Canada and the United States honor their fathers with gifts and cards. It is customary to wear a red or white rose in respect for one's father on Father's Day.

Give dad his own special badge to wear on Father's Day. You might like to pin it to the inside of a card you give him.

Draw a portrait of dad with a bow tie cut from gift wrap paper, or put dad in the news by covering a sheet of construction paper with a page from the newspaper.

Either idea is simple to make and will delight your dad on his special day.

JUNE

Father's Day Pocket

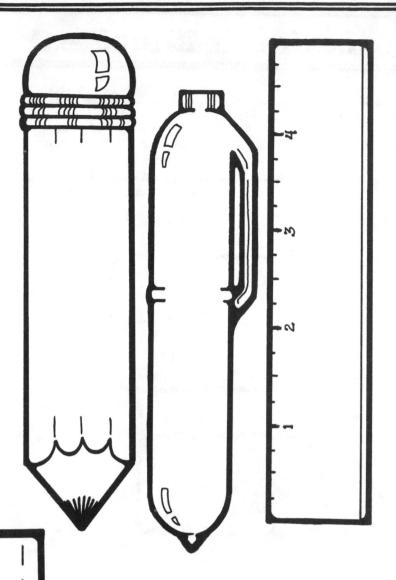

Make a Father's Day gift by cutting two pockets from construction paper. Glue or staple three edges of the pocket together and add your own Father's Day greeting.

List various chores, on the pencil, pen and ruler, that you would like to do for dad on this special day. Place these things inside the pocket.

Father's Day Card

Children will love giving their fathers this simple to make tie for Father's Day.

Fold a 18" X 4" strip of construction paper into thirds. Use the tie pattern to cut the shape accurately. Cut a "V" in the bottom of the tie, as shown. Now, cut two small rectangles from white construction paper and glue them to the top of the tie. Children can add their own Father's Day greetings and designs to the tie. (Patterned wallpaper also works especially well.)

JUNE

My Dad is Special!

My Dad is special because

_____

_____

_____

_____

_____

I like it when my Dad _____

_____

My Dad can do many things! I think he's best at _____

_____

_____

My Dad has a great smile! I like to make him smile by

_____

_____

My Dad is as handsome as a _____

_____

My Dad is smart! He even knows _____

_____

_____

Signed _____ Date _____

JUNE

Happy Father's Day

This is to certify that
my Dad is   the greatest!

because: _____

_____

Love, _____

MY SPECIAL
FATHER'S DAY
PLEDGE!
I PROMISE TO....

1. _____

With all my love!   2. _____

_____ 3. _____

    JUNE

F
A
T
H
E
R

_____
_____
_____
_____
_____
_____
_____
_____
_____
_____
_____
_____

My Dad's the greatest because.....

_____
_____
_____
_____
_____

A Letter to Dad

JUNE

Family and Friends

- FRIENDSHIP ACTIVITIES

- FRIENDSHIP QUESTIONNAIRE

- MY MEMORY BOOK

- U.S.S. FRIENDSHIP

- THE FAMILY

- SPECIAL MESSAGES

- MY FAMILY TREE

- COAT OF ARMS

JUNE

Friendship

Friendship can be found right next door or as far away as the other side of the world. All who search will discover the precious gift of friendship everywhere, even in unexpected places.

A smile is all you need to find a friend. When a smile is returned, you know you've found a new friend.

Try some of these friendship activities with your students.

SECRET PALS

Have each child choose a secret pal by way of a secret drawing. Tell your students that for one week, they should do something nice for their pal, each day. You'll be surprised at the variety of ways they choose to treat their pal, such as, secret notes, artwork, poems, edible treats, etc. At the end of the week, have the pals reveal their identities. You might like to include an inexpensive gift exchange.

CLASS AUTOGRAPH BOOK

Every student in class can be included in this activity by creating just one autograph book. Write one child's name, boldly, at the top of each page of the book. During free time, students can write positive comments about each student, on their page. Students will love seeing what other students have written about them. It will also be a wonderful memento that you can keep for years to come.

NAME POEMS

Have all students exchange names. Ask them to write the person's name, long ways, on a piece of paper. Using the first letter of each line, have them write a poem about the other person, as in this example.

A ngel eyes with soft brown hair,
N ice to be with, really cares.
D ependable and fun in play,
Y es, I hope you stay that way!

LIFE-SIZE FRIENDS

Ask students to pick partners and have them trace each other's complete shape on a large piece of butcher paper. The children can add a face and clothes that best resemble their "new friend." After the figures are painted and cut-out, display them on a class bulletin board, entitled "Life-Size Friends!"

Children will love guessing who is who.

Friendship Questionnaire

Answer each of the "friendship" questions below. You might want to rank your answers by putting a #1 by your first choice, #2 by your second, and so on. Discuss your answers with other students in your class.

1. What do you look for most in a good friend.

    a. appearance
    b. honesty
    c. willingness to share
    d. kindness to others

2. What do you dislike most in a friend.

    a. tells lies
    b. cheats
    c. makes fun of others
    d. takes things that don't belong to him

3. If your friend had done something wrong and someone else was blamed for it, would you;

    a. Say nothing and let the other person get in trouble.
    b. Tell that your friend was really responsible.
    c. Try to convince your friend to tell the truth.

4. If your friend asked you to do something that you knew was wrong, should you;

    a. Go ahead and do it because he's your friend.
    b. Simply refuse to do it.
    c. Explain to him why it is wrong and try to change his mind.

5. If your friend bought a new outfit that he thought was terrific but you thought it looked terrible, would you;

    a. Tell him how bad it really looks.
    b. Tell him it looks great, even though you know it doesn't.
    c. Gently suggest some things that might make it look better.

"MAKE NEW FRIENDS BUT KEEP THE OLD. ONE IS SILVER AND THE OTHER GOLD!"

YEARBOOK MEMORIES

YEAR _____

SCHOOL _____

MY NAME _____

more autographs

JUNE

my Favorite Things

I really enjoyed the _____ grade!

Here is a list of some of my favorite things!

SCHOOL SUBJECT _____

LIBRARY BOOK _____

PLAYGROUND GAME _____

FIELD TRIP _____

ART ACTIVITY _____

EDUCATIONAL FILM _____

FOOD FOR LUNCH _____

Special people at my School!

Principal _____

Teacher _____

Secretary _____

School Nurse _____

Custodian _____

Bus Driver _____

Other people who help me at school:

_____

_____

Names & Addresses

Name _____
Address _____
Phone _____

Name _____
Address _____
Phone _____

Name _____
Address _____
Phone _____

Name _____
Address _____
Phone _____

Name _____
Address _____
Phone _____

Name _____
Address _____
Phone _____

Name _____
Address _____
Phone _____

Name _____
Address _____
Phone _____

My School Picture

Comment from my teacher!

_____
_____
_____
_____
_____
_____

JUNE

Autographs

I remember when......

"TEACHER'S FRIEND" ©

JUNE

Each student can make his own "U.S.S. Friendship" mobile using these simple patterns. Cut the patterns from construction paper and assemble with thread or yarn, as shown. For best results, paste the "Friendship" pattern to posterboard.

Discuss with your class the different qualities needed for being a "best" friend. Ask the students to reflect on the meaning of "friendship. They might discover that they not only have best friends their own age, but that grownups can be best friends, also. They may want to include the names of a neighbor, the school nurse or one of their grandparents to their list of names of best friends.

The "U.S.S. Friendship" pattern can also be used as a booklet cover for reports on friendship or autograph books.

OTHER "FRIENDSHIP" ACTIVITIES:

1. Make a class mural in the theme of "Friendship." Have students illustrate their own ideas of love, peace, respect, etc. Display the mural on the class bulletin board.

2. Older children may like to ponder the problems nations have in becoming good friends. Ask them to think of solutions to those problems, such as; reducing nuclear weapons, feeding the hungry and establishing equality for all people. Have them present their ideas to the class for discussion.

FRIENDSHIP IS....

_____
_____
_____
_____
_____
_____
_____
_____
_____
_____

How I can be a best friend.

_____
_____
_____
_____
_____
_____
_____
_____
_____
_____

What I look for in a friend.

_____
_____
_____
_____
_____
_____
_____
_____
_____
_____
_____
_____

My special friends:

_____
_____
_____
_____
_____
_____
_____
_____
_____
_____
_____

JUNE

The Family ♡ ✿ ♡ ✿ ♡ ✿

The family unit has always played an important role in the foundation of our country and heritage. The way family members relate to one another helps in forming the way we also view ourselves.

Point out to your students that all families are different and that each family has many things of which to be proud. Ask each student to think about the wonderful qualities each member contributes to the family and home. Encourage your students to find ways to compliment family members. Ask them to look for things in which they can say thank you and show their gratitude. They may like to write a note to each member of the family telling them how much they're admired and appreciated.

Complete this family questionnaire.

♡ 1. My family loves to _____

_____

✿ 2. My favorite family holiday is _____

We celebrate it by _____

_____

♡ 3. When something wonderful happens in our family we usually _____

_____

✿ 4. Our family shows how much we love each other by _____

_____

♡ 5. My family is special because _____

_____

✿ 6. Here is a list of my family members and what I most admire about each one!

_____   _____

_____   _____

_____   _____

_____   _____

_____   _____

Special Messages

A Note to Mom, _____

_____

_____

_____

_____

A Note to Dad, _____

_____

_____

_____

_____

A Note to My Sister, _____

_____

_____

_____

_____

A Note to My Brother, _____

_____

_____

_____

_____

JUNE

My Family Tree

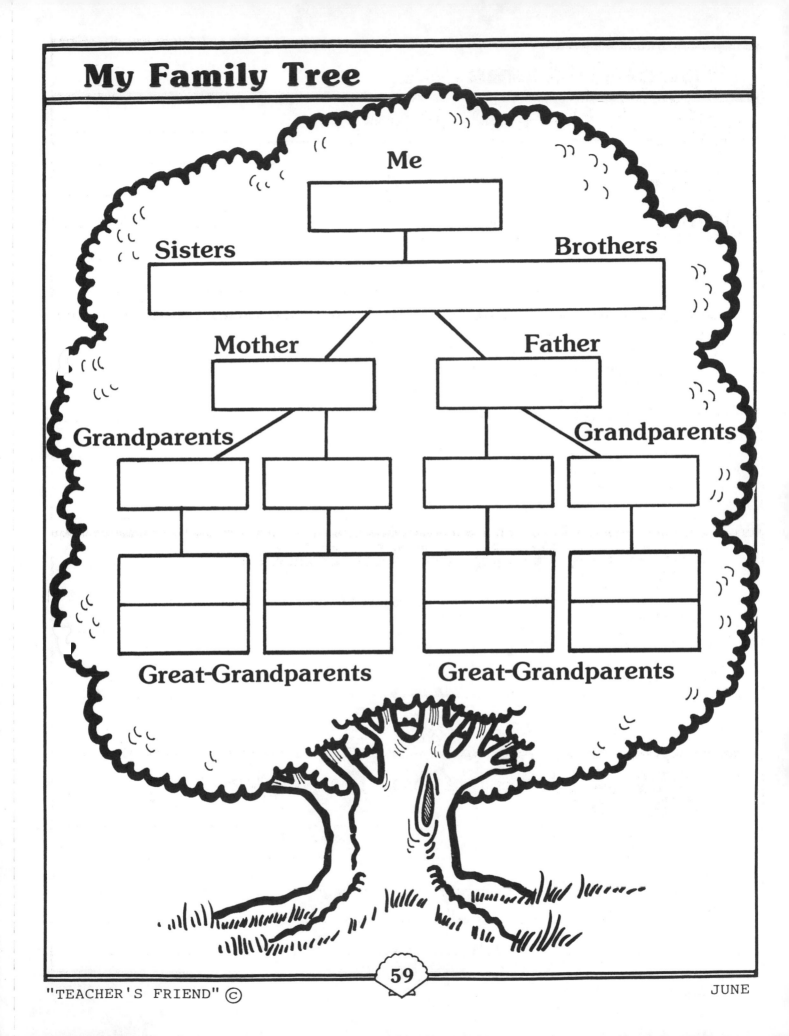

Me

Sisters   Brothers

Mother   Father

Grandparents   Grandparents

Great-Grandparents   Great-Grandparents

Coat of Arms

Students will love creating their own personal or family Coat of Arms. Make copies of the shield pattern from colored construction paper and have each child illustrate the four areas of the shield.

INITIALS - Children can design their own initials and draw them in the appropriate space. They may like to use fluorescent colors or glitter on the letters.

ACCOMPLISHMENTS - Students can draw pictures illustrating their many acccomplishments or they may simply want to list them.

MOTTO - Ask the children to think of different values that mean a great deal to them. Have them formulate these thoughts into short statements. They might like it to be a rule by which to live or a special quality they wish to express.

GOALS - Have your students think of goals they would like their families or themselves to accomplish. Ask them to illustrate these ideals.

Display the Coat of Arms on the class bulletin board. Children may like to add a variety of decorations to their shields.

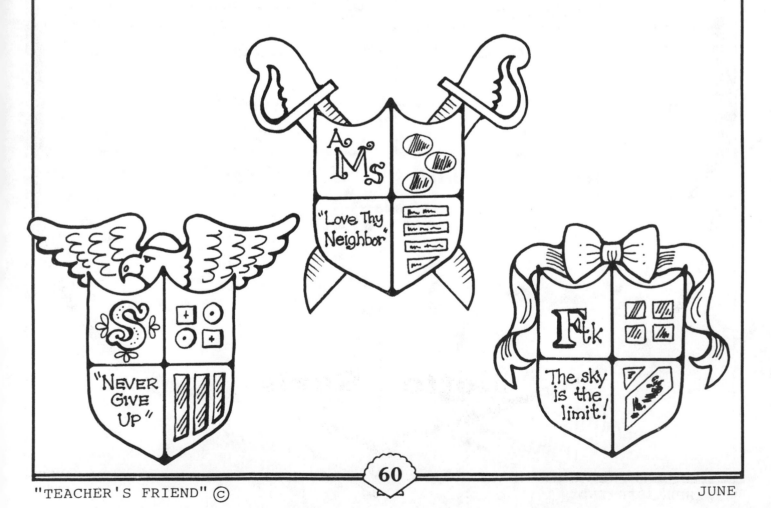

Coat of Arms

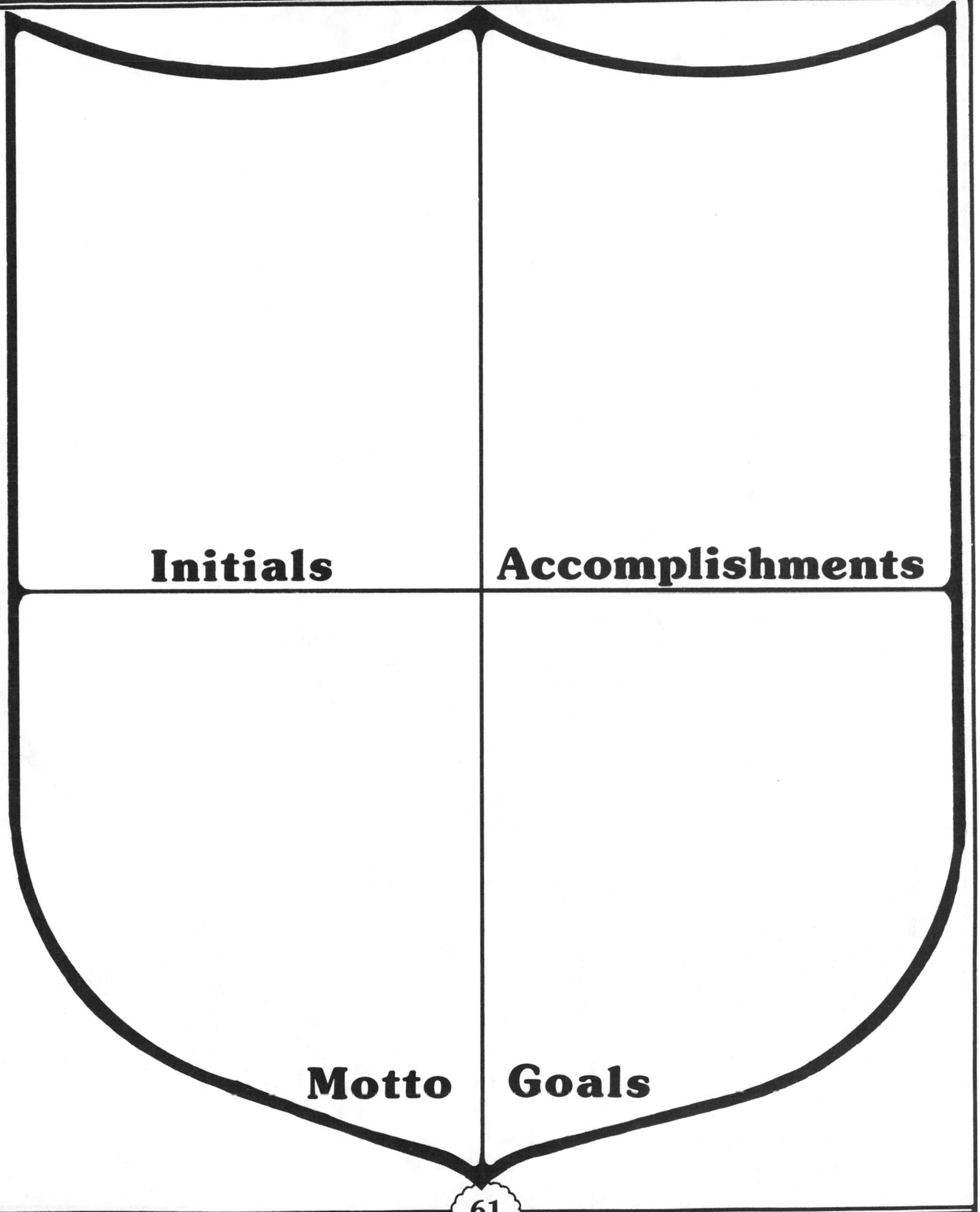

Initials

Accomplishments

Motto Goals

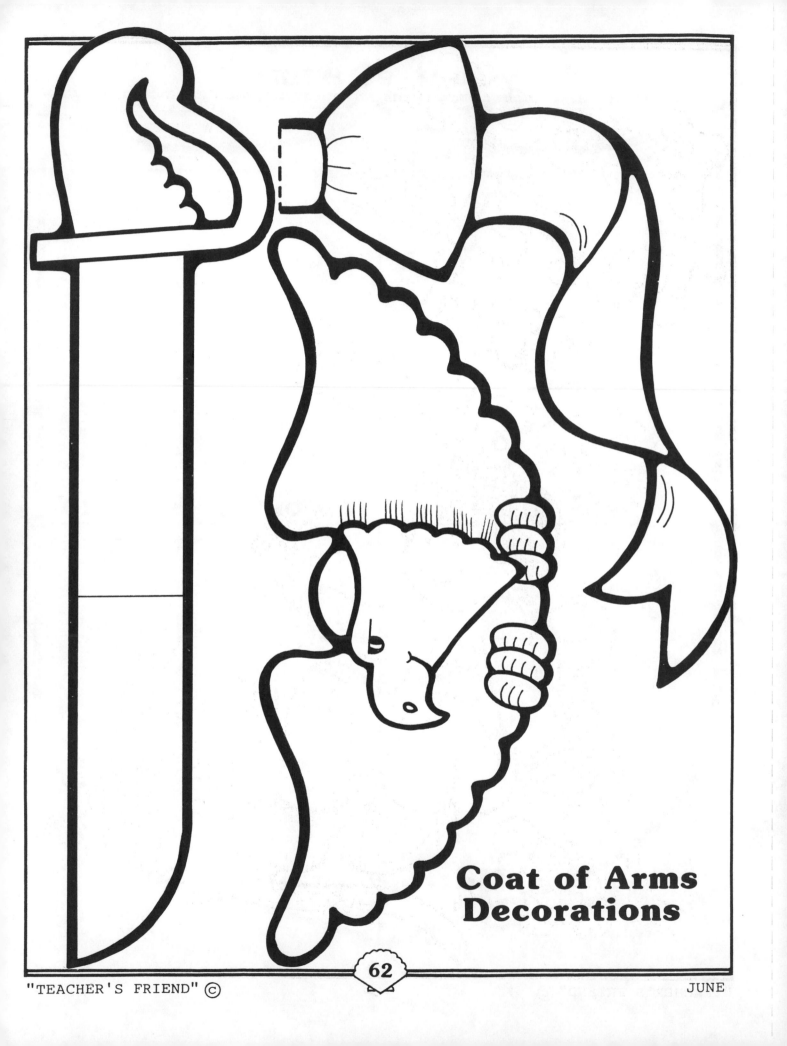

Coat of Arms Decorations

JUNE

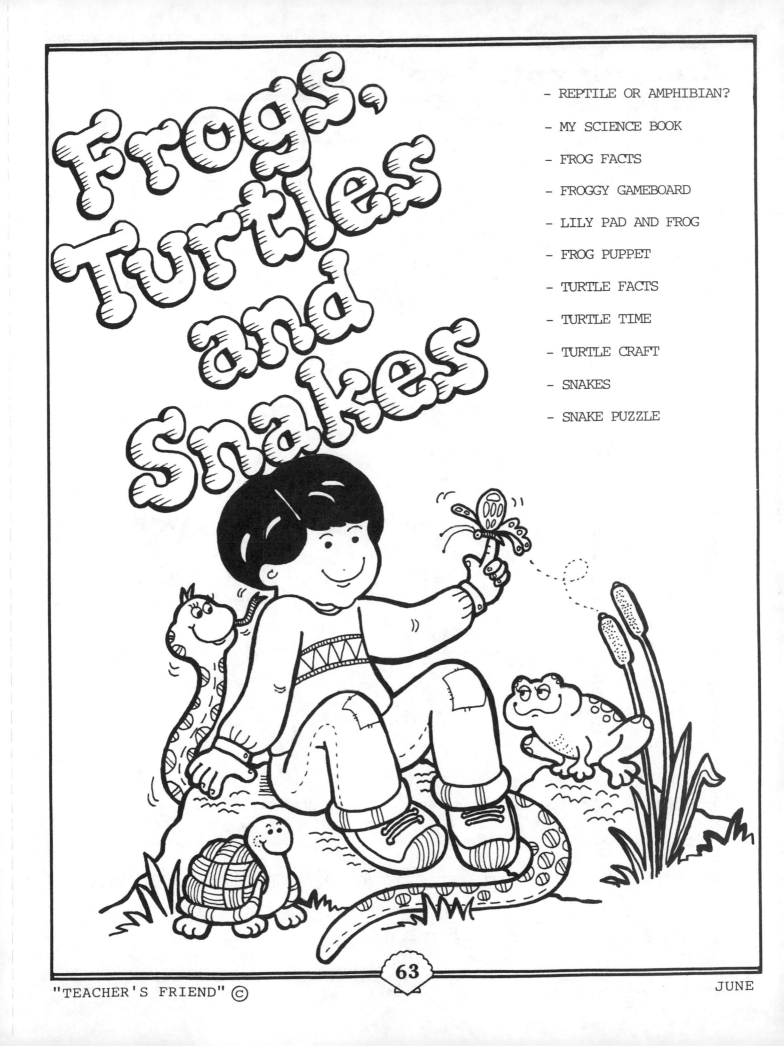

Frogs, Turtles and Snakes

- REPTILE OR AMPHIBIAN?
- MY SCIENCE BOOK
- FROG FACTS
- FROGGY GAMEBOARD
- LILY PAD AND FROG
- FROG PUPPET
- TURTLE FACTS
- TURTLE TIME
- TURTLE CRAFT
- SNAKES
- SNAKE PUZZLE

Reptile and Amphibian Fun

ACTIVITY 3

UNSCRAMBLE THESE REPTILE AND AMPHIBIAN WORDS!

leturt _ _ _ _ _ _

skena _ _ _ _ _

grof _ _ _ _

adot _ _ _ _

toraglila _ _ _ _ _ _ _ _ _

zildar _ _ _ _ _ _

colideroc _ _ _ _ _ _ _ _ _

trtooise _ _ _ _ _ _ _ _

ANSWER THESE QUESTIONS.   ACTIVITY 4

1. Frogs start life as _ _ _ _ _ _ _ _.

2. Frogs and toads are _ _ _ _ _ _ _ _ _ _.

3. Most water turtles are _ _ _ _ eaters.

4. Land turtles are _ _ _ _ _ eaters.

5. Some tortoises can live to be _ _ _ years old.

6. All turtles lay _ _ _ _.

7. All reptiles are _ _ _ _ -blooded.

8. Snakes have no _ _ _ _.

9. Turtles, crocodiles, lizards and snakes are _ _ _ _ _ _ _ _.

This is what I've learned about reptiles and amphibians:

_____

_____

_____

_____

JUNE

Reptile or Amphibian?

Select an animal that is either reptile or amphibian. Complete the following sentences.

The name of my animal is _____

It lives in _____

My animal is different than other animals because _____

_____

_____

_____

The life cycle of my animal is very interesting. This is what happens:

_____

_____

_____

_____

Here is a drawing of my animal.   My animal feeds on _____

_____

Another fascinating fact is _____

_____

_____

_____

My animal is: A REPTILE
                A AMPHIBIAN

JUNE

My
Science
Book

Name

JUNE

Frog Facts

Your students will love observing the life-cycle of the frog in the class-room. Tadpoles can be raised in a glass aquarium. Later, when the frogs have fully developed, you will want to build a vivarium.

Your vivarium can be built with a wooden frame measuring about four feet long, two feet wide and two feet high. The box should be covered with a fine wire screen. Place your vivarium outside in a semi-shaded area. It should contain a good supply of water. (A kitchen dish-pan, filled with pond water, will work fine.) Make sure to include plenty of rocks, small logs, and green plants to provide shelter for the frogs. You might have to collect insects for your frogs to eat.

Name _____

Frog Facts

Frogs and toads may look alike but it's easy to tell them apart. Frogs have smooth, slippery, soft skin. Toads have rough, warty skin.

Frogs and toads are amphibians. This means that they live on both land and in the water.

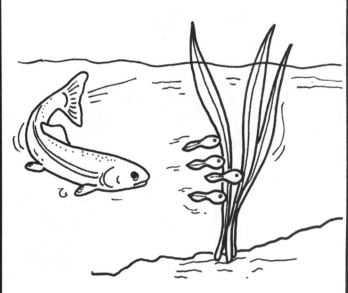

The mother frog lays her eggs near vegetation in a pond of water.

The eggs hatch into tiny tadpoles that breathe with gills and feed on plants in the water.

JUNE

Frog Facts

Tadpoles become fast swimmers, using their fish-like tail to propel them through the water.

Soon the tadpoles begin to change. Small back legs are the first to appear. Next, the front legs begin to develop.

As the tadpoles grow, the tails become shorter and shorter. At last the change is complete.

From now on, the new little frog will spend some of his time on land. Now, his main source of food is insects.

JUNE

JUNE

Help Froggy get to land!

TEACHERS: Two, three or four children can play this game. Make your own task cards or write math problems, that must be solved, on each lily pad.

Lily Pad and Frog

This cute frog and lily pad can easily be used to organize class monitors or reading groups. For reading groups, enlarge the pad and place several frogs around the name of the group.

Mike
CLEAN UP

Cindy
FLAG SALUTE

JUNE

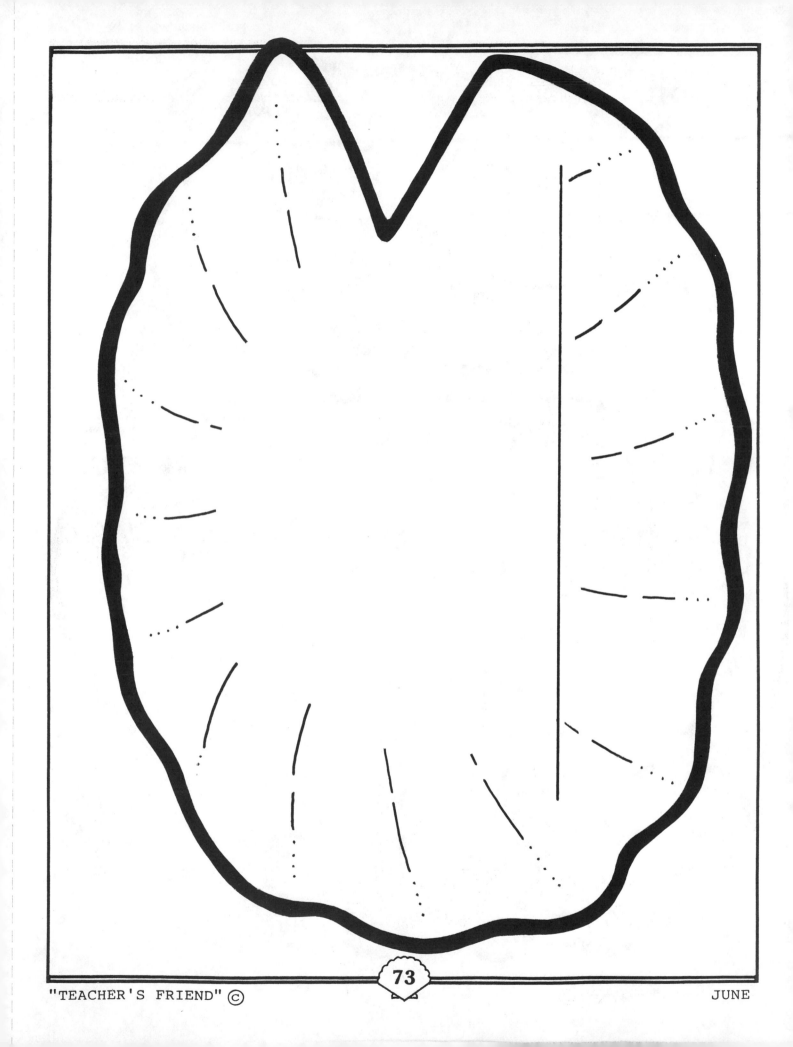

JUNE

Frog Puppet

JUNE

Turtle Facts

Turtles and tortoises are fascinating animals. They are some of the oldest on earth. Scientists have found fossils dating as far back as 2,000 years ago. That means that turtles and tortoises survived the extinction of the dinosuars.

There are many types of turtles; freshwater turtles, soft-shelled turtles, snapping turtles, sea turtles and tortoises. (You might like to have your students collect pictures of different turtles and ask them to research the various species.)

Turtles can also be included in your vivarium with your frogs. Turtles are carniverous or meat eaters. You will need to provide fresh meat such as worms, fish, shredded meat and occasionally liver. Tortoises eat lettuce, cauliflower, fruit and dandelions.

Select two or three children to monitor the vivarium. They can be responsible for changing the water and providing the food. New monitors should be chosen every few weeks to provide an opportunity for everyone to help.

Name _____

Turtle Facts

There are many different kinds of turtles. However, they all have one thing in common, a shell. This is the one thing that makes them unique to other reptiles.

Some turtles live in water and some on land. Land turtles are often called tortoises. They live to be a hundred years old and can grow to more than one thousand pounds.

Most water turtles are meat eaters. They feed on small fish. The land turtles are vegetarians and eat only plants.

A box turtle can pull his head, legs and tail into his shell, completely protecting himself.

JUNE

Turtle Facts

If a box turtle gets turned upside down, he has a very hard time turning himself over again.

All turtles lay their eggs on land. The mother digs a hole in soft dirt or sand. She lays her eggs in the hole and then covers them with dirt.

The mother turtle then leaves her eggs to incubate in the warm sunshine, never to return.

The eggs hatch in about three months. The little turtles have to struggle to break through the tough shells of the eggs.

JUNE

Turtle Time

A variety of matching activities can easily be made with this cute turtle character by simply cutting several squares of colored paper. Ask your students to match the squares to the squares on the turtle's shell. Try matching ordinal numbers, contractions, time or multiplication problems.

JUNE

Turtle Craft

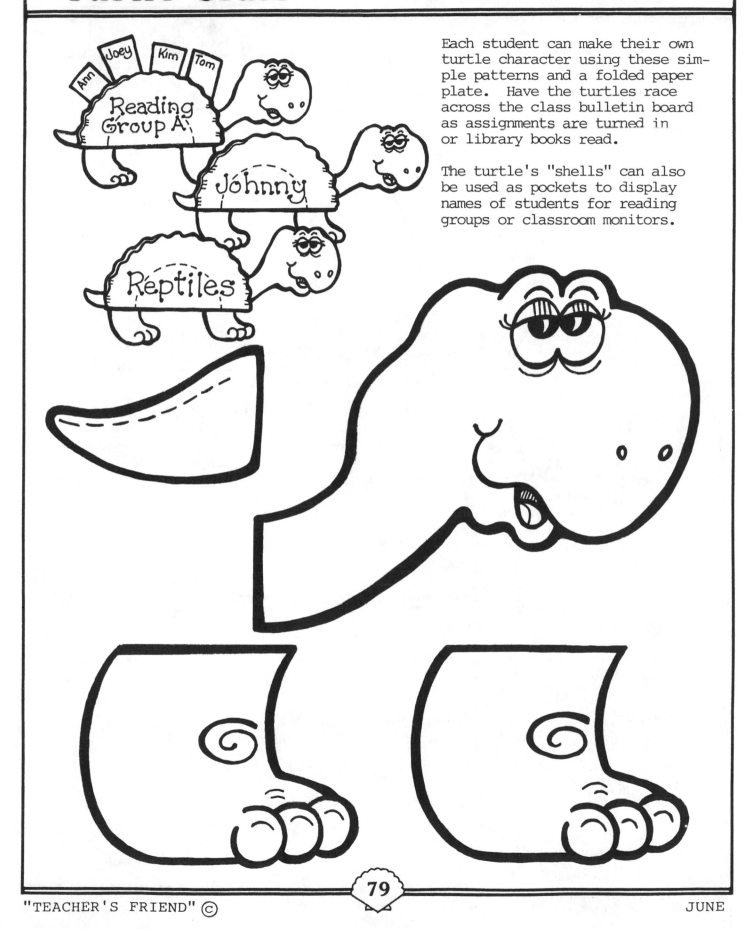

Each student can make their own turtle character using these simple patterns and a folded paper plate. Have the turtles race across the class bulletin board as assignments are turned in or library books read.

The turtle's "shells" can also be used as pockets to display names of students for reading groups or classroom monitors.

Ann Joey Kim Tom

Reading Group A

Johnny

Reptiles

JUNE

Snakes

Dinosaurs ruled the earth for more than 100 million years, then they mysteriously disappeared. Only five types of reptiles have survived to present day; turtles, crocodilians, lizards, the lizard-like tuataras and snakes.

Unlike other reptiles, snakes have no legs. Instead they walk with their ribs. A snake has many small bones that connect together to form their backbone. Therefore, they can bend it very easily. By wiggling from side to side, a snake travels rather easily.

All reptiles, including snakes, are cold-blooded. This means that their temperature rises and falls with the temperature of the air around them. You can often find snakes sunning themselves on rocks in the springtime. This is their way of raising the temperature of their bodies.

Snakes, like all reptiles, shed their skin periodically. How often they shed their skin depends on their age, diet and overall health. Snakes shed their skin in one long piece. They crawl out of their old skin, turning it inside out as they go. Young snakes shed their skin more often than older ones because they are growing.

Most snakes are very helpful because they eat small rodents like rats and mice. They also eat harmful insects. The king snake will even eat other poisonous snakes. Snakes search for their food by feeling for vibrations in the ground. They also smell with their tongues. Snakes have poorly developed sight and hearing.

Most snakes hatch their young from eggs, but a few bear their young live. The harmless garter snake is one of these. The mother garter snake carries her eggs in her body until they develop into baby snakes. She then delivers them alive.

Full grown snakes vary from only a few inches long to more than 30 feet. The anaconda is the largest snake known, measuring as long as 38 feet and weighing more than 250 pounds.

Snakes are most common in the warm areas of the world. Where it is cold, snakes must seek protection and hibernate in the winter.

Find out about a snake common in your area. What does it look like? What does it eat? Where does it live?

_____

_____

_____

Snake Puzzle

Teachers: Add your own math problems to the snake.

Cut the snake into sections and have students race to put him together.

JUNE

Creative Writing

_____

_____

_____

_____

_____

_____

_____

_____

_____

_____

_____

_____

_____

_____

_____

_____

_____

_____

_____

_____

_____

_____

_____

_____

JUNE

Oceanography

- WHALE WRITING
- MOVABLE OCTOPUS
- PIRATE COSTUME
- PIRATE STORY

- FISH PATTERNS
- WHALE OF A WHEEL
- INTERNATIONAL CHILDREN
- OCTOPUS PUPPET

Fish Patterns

Use these cute fish patterns as field trip name tags or enlarge them on poster board and display them as a clever bulletin board theme.

JUNE

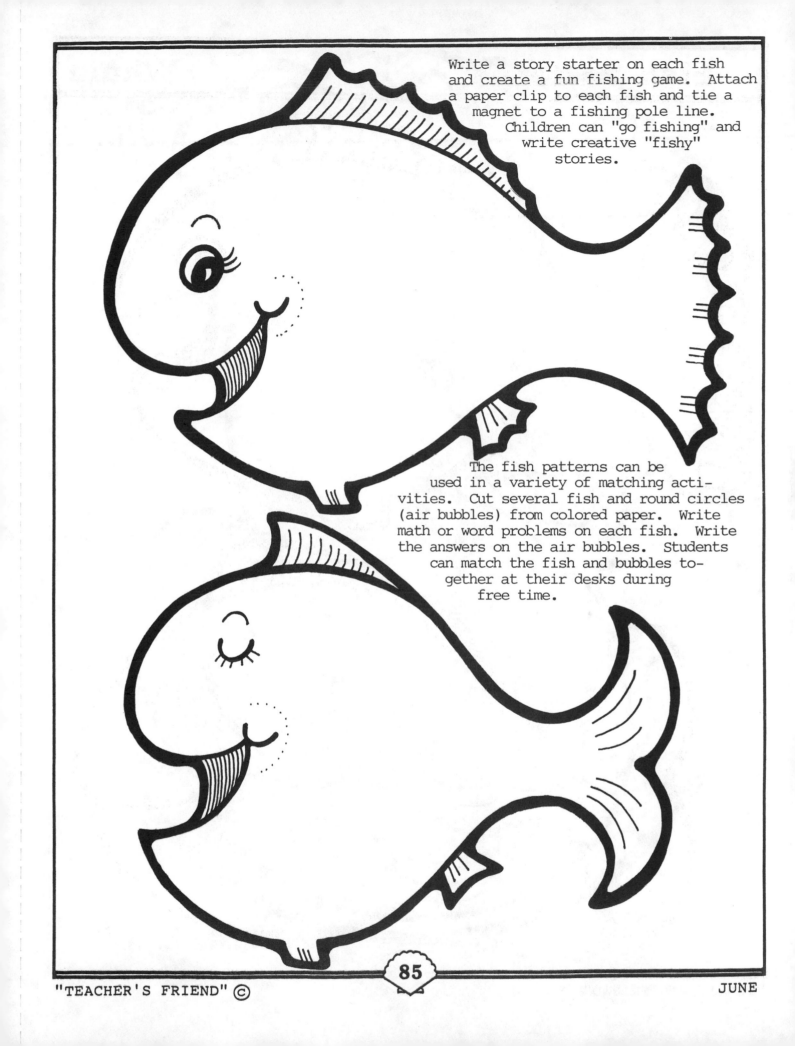

Write a story starter on each fish and create a fun fishing game. Attach a paper clip to each fish and tie a magnet to a fishing pole line. Children can "go fishing" and write creative "fishy" stories.

The fish patterns can be used in a variety of matching activities. Cut several fish and round circles (air bubbles) from colored paper. Write math or word problems on each fish. Write the answers on the air bubbles. Students can match the fish and bubbles together at their desks during free time.

85

Whale of a Wheel

CUT OUT

CUT OUT

JUNE

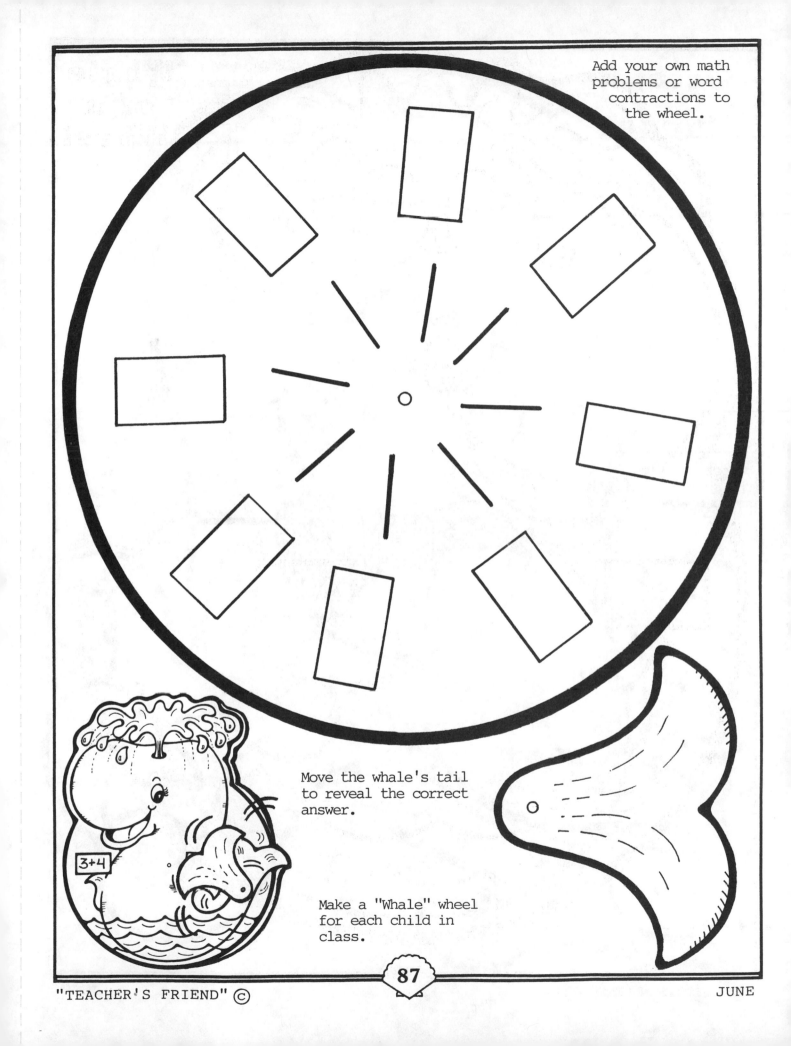

Add your own math problems or word contractions to the wheel.

Move the whale's tail to reveal the correct answer.

Make a "Whale" wheel for each child in class.

3+4

"TEACHER'S FRIEND" ©   JUNE

Octopus Puppet

Cut this puppet from construction paper. Glue the two pieces to a small brown lunch bag.

Use the octopus puppet to teach the short vowell sound of the letter "O."

JUNE

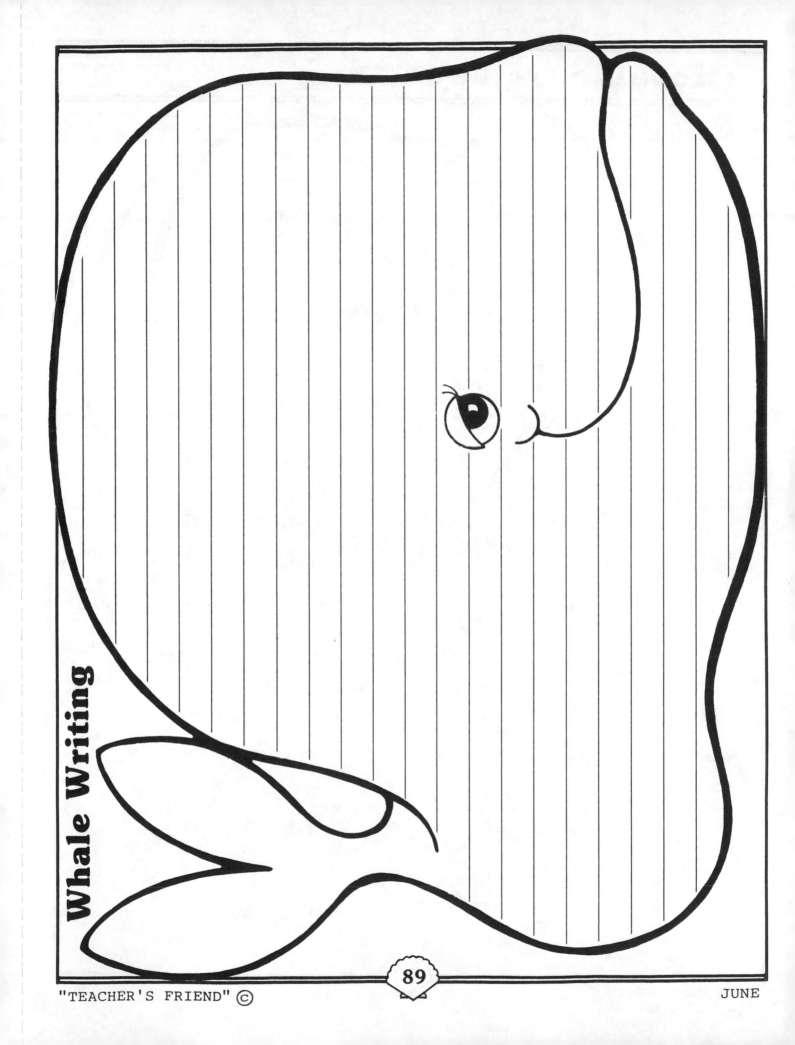

Whale Writing

JUNE

Movable Octopus

Cut one octopus pattern from construction or index paper. Cut four copies of each arm. Color with markers or crayons.

Assemble the legs, as shown, and attach with a brass fastener.

Students will love moving his arms or displaying him on the class bulletin board.

JUNE

"TEACHER'S FRIEND" ©   JUNE

JUNE

Creative Writing

Pirate Fun

Along with the study of oceanography, your students will love participating in a fun unit of pirate activities.

Draw a large pirate map on the class bulletin board. Students can be divided into teams and their progress charted as oceanography reports are turned in, library books read, or multiplication facts learned. Each team can be racing toward a large treasure chest filled with gift certificates or maybe "pieces of eight."

A scavenger hunt, around the school grounds, can top off the event. The children can return to class to find buccaneer cookies and pirate grog for refreshments.

Pirate Costume

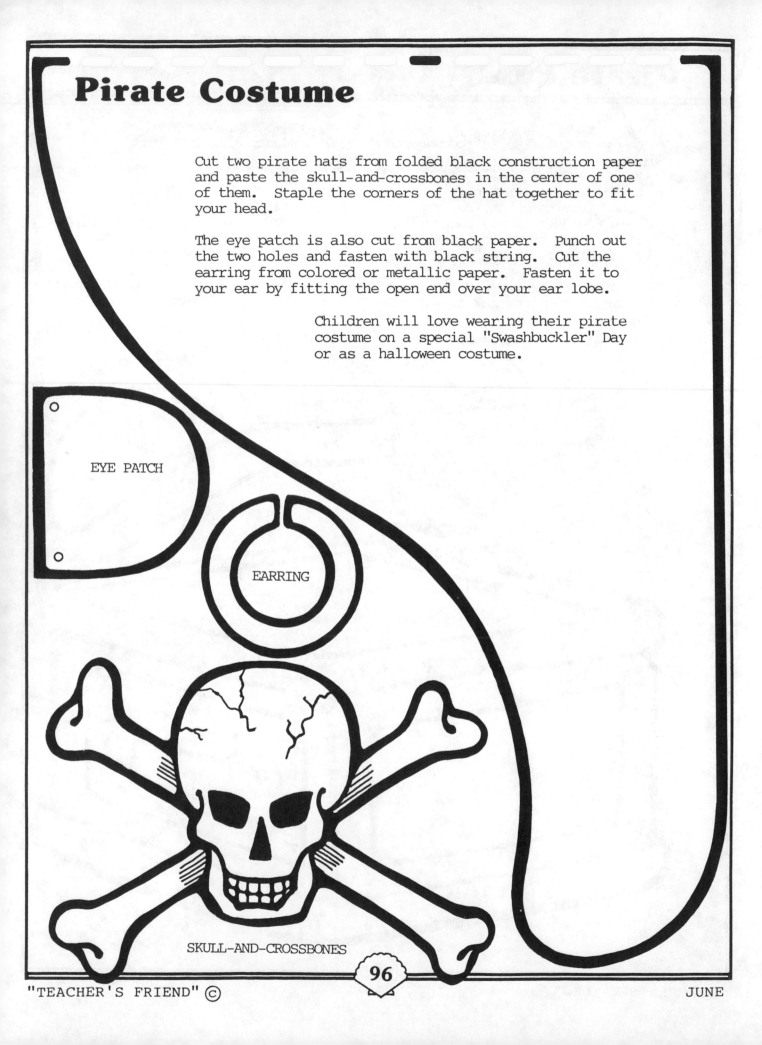

Cut two pirate hats from folded black construction paper and paste the skull-and-crossbones in the center of one of them. Staple the corners of the hat together to fit your head.

The eye patch is also cut from black paper. Punch out the two holes and fasten with black string. Cut the earring from colored or metallic paper. Fasten it to your ear by fitting the open end over your ear lobe.

Children will love wearing their pirate costume on a special "Swashbuckler" Day or as a halloween costume.

EYE PATCH

EARRING

SKULL-AND-CROSSBONES

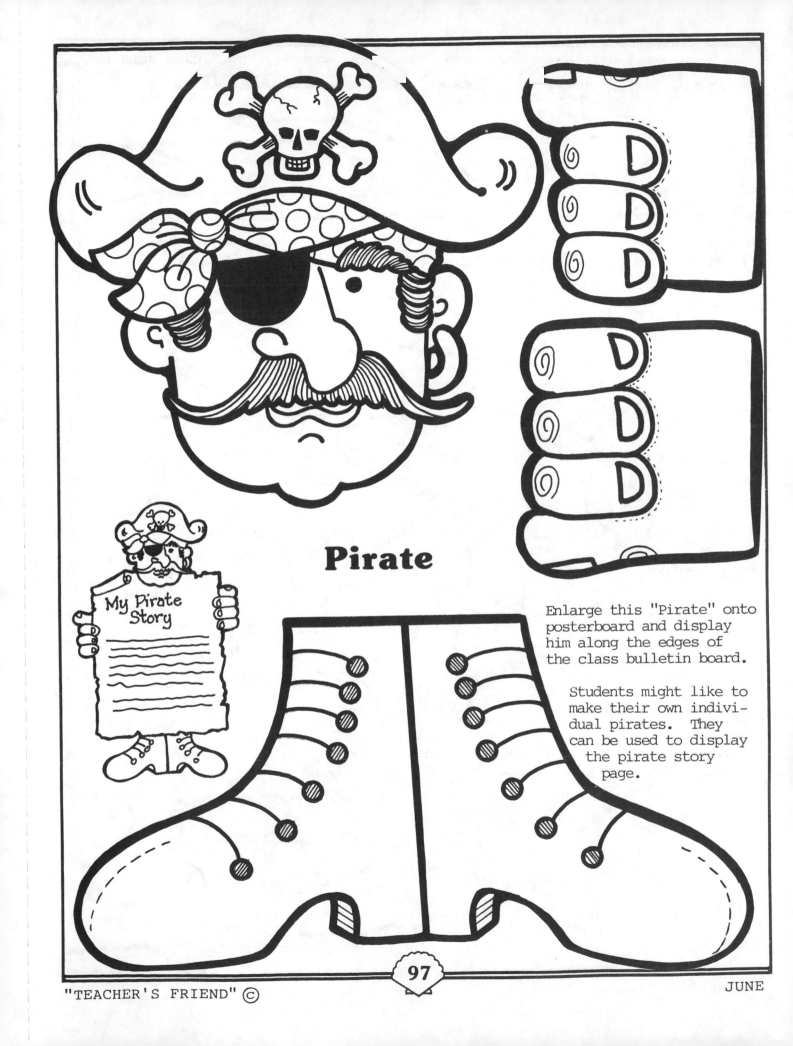

Pirate

Enlarge this "Pirate" onto posterboard and display him along the edges of the class bulletin board.

Students might like to make their own individual pirates. They can be used to display the pirate story page.

My Pirate Story

Pirate Gameboard

TEACHERS: Two, three or four children can play this game. Make your own oceanography task cards.

JUNE

My Pirate Story

JUNE

Bulletin Boards and more!

Rob

Ann Mary

Andy Joey Sue

Sally Mike Toni

Kacie Jim Dee

Turtle Tales by Room 14

"TEACHER'S FRIEND" ©

JUNE

THE FUTURE IS OURS!

Display a large graduate character on the class bulletin board. Cut the cap and gown from black butcher paper and make a tassle from colored yarn.

Students can write papers about their goals for the future or maybe just next year.

START A SUMMER HOBBY!

Cut a giant sun from yellow butcher paper and pin it to the bulletin board. Ask students to list different hobbies that they might enjoy doing this summer.

Write the various hobbies around the sun, as shown.

FRIENDSHIP

Emphasize respect for one another by displaying this striking "hands" bulletin board. Enlarge the hands, as shown, using butcher paper. Or, you may wish to make a chain of clasping hands reaching from one end of the room to the other.

and more....

LEAP INTO LEARNING!

Paper bag frog puppets will leap off the bulletin board with this clever idea. Ask each student to make their own frog puppet and display the best ones on the board along with paper lily pads and cattails.

WHAT A CATCH!

Display this cute fisherman on the class bulletin board. Give each student a copy of the fish pattern and ask them to write a "fishy" story. Pin the fish stories to the end of his fishing pole, as shown.

WE'RE MATH SHARKS

Cut several sharks from colored butcher paper. Write word problems on each shark that pertain to these fascinating sea creatures. One example might be; "If this shark eats 30 pounds of fish a day, how much does it eat in one week?" Students can write their answers on the air bubbles.

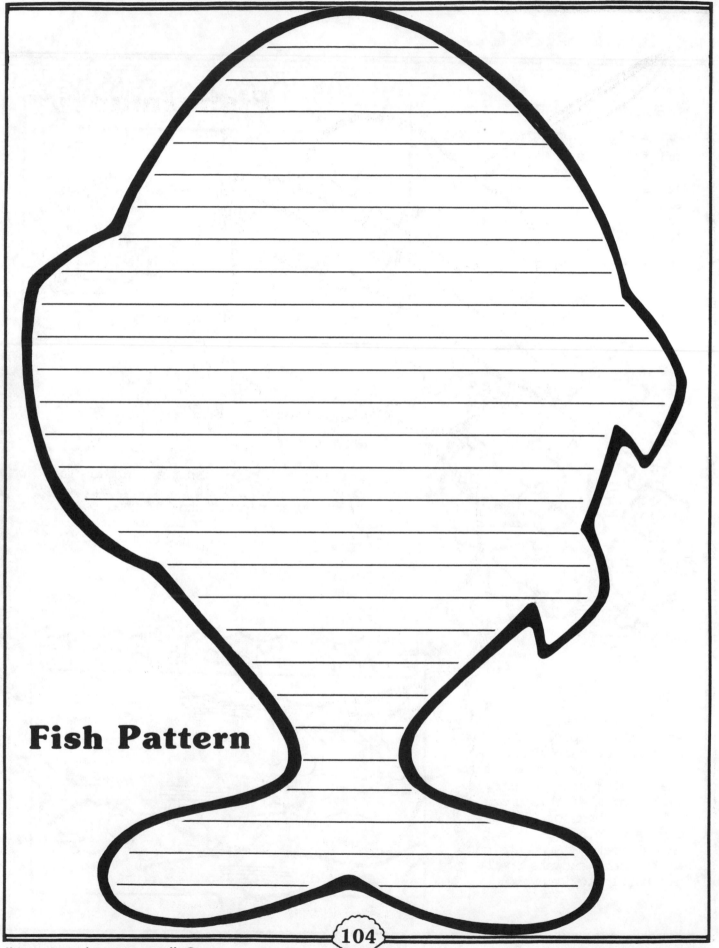

Fish Pattern

Fisherman

JUNE

Symbols of Friendship

JUNE

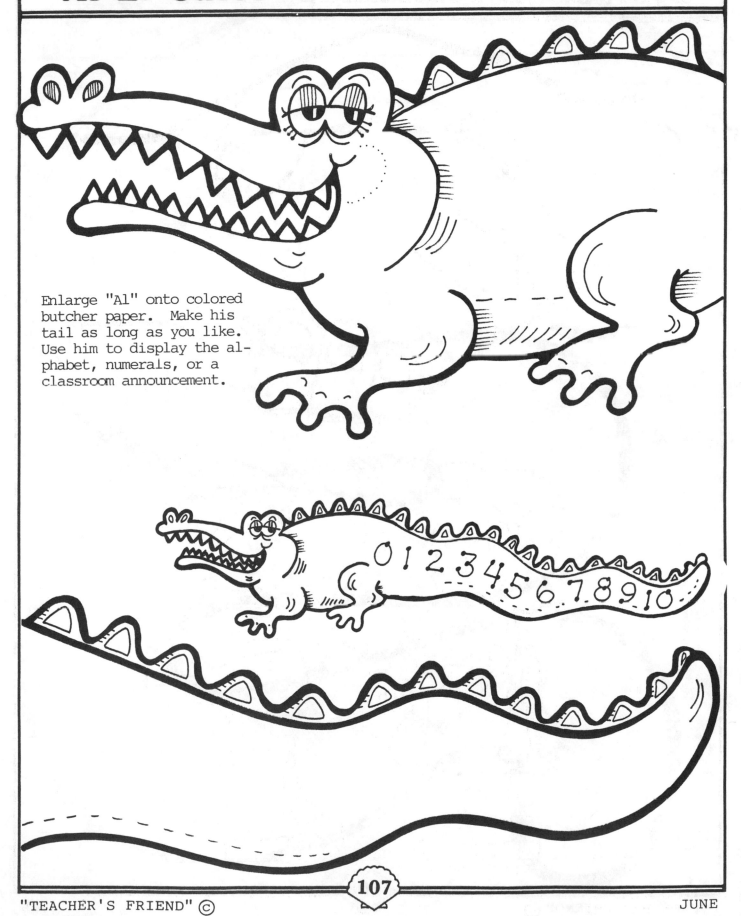

Enlarge "Al" onto colored butcher paper. Make his tail as long as you like. Use him to display the alphabet, numerals, or a classroom announcement.

0 1 2 3 4 5 6 7 8 9 10

Sneaky Snake

Enlarge "Sneaky" onto butcher paper. Make him as long as you wish. Use him to display classroom rules across the top of your bulletin board.

Geraldine Giraffe

Enlarge "Geraldine" onto colored butcher paper. Display her vertically on a blank wall. With a yardstick, mark off feet and inches along her neck. (You can make her neck as long as you wish.) Your students will love to measure themselves and see how much they've grown throughout the school year.

JUNE

Bertha Bird

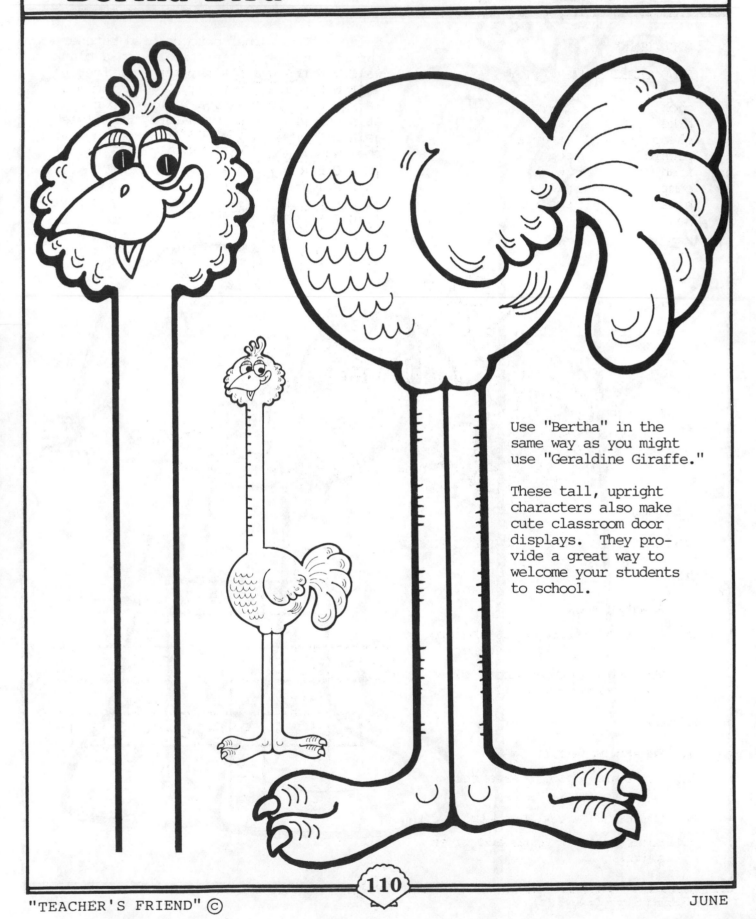

Use "Bertha" in the same way as you might use "Geraldine Giraffe."

These tall, upright characters also make cute classroom door displays. They provide a great way to welcome your students to school.

Answer Key

ACTIVITY 1

FIND THESE SUMMER ACTIVITIES:

cook	skate
bike	garden
sleep	explore
picnic	boat
fish	swim
camp	play
hike	sports
sew	

```
S C V G F S W I M K L O P L K J H F T Y
L A W E D F R S D R F T L D E R F G H Y
E S C O O K S D F G T Y A D S P O R T S
E S W E R A E S W D F R Y W S T Y U I O
P A E D R F W E X P L O R E D T Y U K M
I S W G A R D E N D G T Y H B O A T E R
C W Q E R T Y U A W E R T Y H G F D S T
N F R T Y U H J H D F T Y G H U I J K L
I D R F G T I F F I S H F T Y U I O P V
C B I K E D K V G T Y H N M K I O L R E
A X C G T Y E C A M P D V G T Y H N M J
A W E D S C F R T G B H Y U J M N K I O
A S D F G T Y H J K I O S K A T E D R T
X C Z V B G F D S A Z X B N M J K H F D
```

ACTIVITY 2

COMPLETE THIS SUMMER CROSSWORD PUZZLE

DOWN

1. A water sport

2. You should always look before you _ _ _ _ into the water!

3. To keep your head above water and remain very still.

ACROSS

4. Something wet.

5. All swimmers must have strong _ _ _ _.

6. Swimmers kick with their _ _ _ _.

7. Someone who watches and saves swimmers.

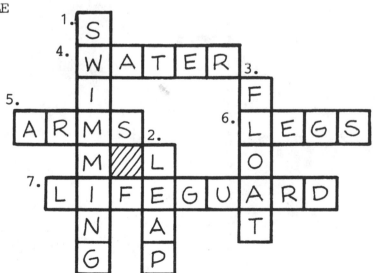

Answer Key

ACTIVITY 3

UNSCRAMBLE THESE REPTILE AND AMPHIBIAN WORDS!

leturt   turtle
skena   snake
grof   frog
adot   toad
toraglila   alligator
zildar   lizard
colideroc   crocodile
trtooise   tortoise

ANSWER THESE QUESTIONS.   ACTIVITY 4

1. Frogs start life as tadpoles.

2. Frogs and toads are amphibians.

3. Most water turtles are meat eaters.

4. Land turtles are plant eaters.

5. Some tortouises can live to be 100 years old.

6. All turtles lay eggs.

7. All reptiles are cold-blooded.

8. Snakes have no legs.

9. Turtles, crocodiles, lizards and snakes are reptiles.

JUNE